What People Are Saying About Cortney Westbrook

THE PEOPLE'S ENTREPRENEUR

Working with The People's Entrepreneur has been such a pleasure. He took my ideas and turned them into works of art. Any time I had any problems with my website or print media, he was quick to solve them for me and even help me through them. Everyone who has made comments about our website, has only said how awesome it looked. I will continue to use Cortney for all of my design projects.

-Johnette Bramlett

One day I was at home flipping through the TV channels and came across The People's Entrepreneur on a TV show. Listening to him talk really inspired me to start back using the talents that God blessed me with. I love to write and it comes natural to me, but so much has been going on in my life and around me that I just let it go. One of my dreams has been to write a book. After hearing Cortney speak, I know that I have nothing to lose; and who knows, I may write a bestselling book that will inspire someone in some way. God bless Cortney and his wife!

- Anonymous

The People's Entrepreneur equips and empowers individuals to identify their passion and walk out their purpose. He encourages people to never settle for good because greatness is available.

- Wordsmith

I was speechless upon viewing my photos. The People's Entrepreneur, with grace, captured the essence of the moment beautifully; I'm amazed at the power of photography and how it clads with the power of motion, turning reality into precious memory. Thank you, sir!

- Tracey Underwood

I absolutely love the pictures Cortney took of me dancing. I absolutely love them! My friends think that they are amazing shots and that he captured the true essence of ministry versus performing. I have other pictures of me in a production with very scripted choreography, but I must say that I love *these* pictures the most. They're simply beautiful! I am most humbled and grateful for my experience at the showcase and for these pictures. Thank you Cortney.

- LaVawn Scott

Cortney Westbrook is one of the leading voices for entrepreneurs of the millennial generation. His willingness to be selfless and help other entrepreneurs succeed is what earned him the nickname "The People's Entrepreneur". With multiple businesses under his belt and pleased clients by his side, Mr. Westbrook is truly the model for what it looks like to live your life in drive.

- Dwight "Transprent" Taylor, Sr.

STUCK IN NEUTRAL

HOW TO ACHIEVE SUCCESS BY LIVING LIFE IN DRIVE

CORTNEY WESTBROOK

STUCK IN NEUTRAL by Cortney Westbrook
Published by E Squared Publishing Group
E Squared Publishing Group
PO Box 2251
Tupelo, MS 38803
www.livingindrive.com

Unless otherwise noted, all Scripture quotations are from the New King James Version of the Bible.

Copyright © 2015 Cortney Westbrook
All rights reserved.
ISBN-13: 978-1502318831
ISBN-10: 1502318830

Printed in the United States of America

Cover design by E Squared Publishing Group
Cover photography by Lauren Wood

Visit the author's website: www.cortneywestbrook.com

Contents

Acknowledgements   viii

Foreword   .   xii

1   My Journey to Living in Drive   1

2   The Real Way to Find Your True Purpose   9

3   The True Meaning of Your Gift   15

4   The Secret to Getting Ahead is Getting Started   23

5   Don't Believe in Yourself   25

6   Guaranteed Success with God-Confidence   29

7   Building Success with Confidence   33

8   Living a Life of Gratitude   39

9   No Sacrifice, No Success   57

10   Make Adjustments, Not Excuses   61

11   Problems Are Not Stop Signs, They're Guidelines   65

12   Negative + Positive = Power   69

13   Understanding Failure   71

14   The Real Key to Success   81

15   Overcoming Opposition and Negativity   83

ACKNOWLEDGMENTS

Before I take a few moments to acknowledge some important people, I want to first acknowledge my faith. I am unapologetically Christian and I stand firm on my beliefs and will never compromise that. I thank the Lord Jesus Christ for giving me life and purpose. Without the leading of the Holy Spirit I could never do what I do and I would never be where I am today.

No one who achieves success does so without acknowledging the help of others. The wise and confident acknowledge this help with gratitude.
- Alfred North Whitehead

I want to acknowledge my wife Christian. Honey, thank you for always being there for me and for your undying love and support throughout all of these years. You are the best wife and friend a man could ever ask for.

Meeke, thank you so much for everything you've done. Thank you for your support, wisdom, council, coaching and advice. Your friendship is more valuable than words can express. Your contributions are immensely appreciated. You are an invaluable asset to my team, family and life.

Wil, thank you for first being a genuine friend. Thank you for your support personally and professionally. I look forward to continuing to build our lifelong brotherhood. Blessings on you are your family.

Antoine Jackson, thank you for your advice, council, marketing strategies and support in this project. You've been a valuable asset in my corner. I look forward to building with you indefinitely.

Dwight Taylor, I honestly don't know the words to say to you that will accurately express my gratitude, appreciation and love for you brother. You've been there for me when not many people were, personally and professionally. We've grown together over the years and I look forward to our lifelong brotherhood and friendship.

David "Wordsmith" Derf– dude you are a dynamic brother and you're a powerhouse for the Kingdom of God. Thank you so much for your love and support over the years in building this brand. You are the epitome of "going up together" and your life exemplifies that every single day. You *are* The Neighborhood H.O.P.E. Dealer!

Last, but certainly not least, I'd like to thank Melonie Manning. Mel, words can't express how grateful I am to have you in my corner. God has blessed you with a gift and you have no problems flourishing in it. You did a phenomenal job working with me on this book and I am 100% happy, pleased and satisfied. I look forward to working with you in the future and building a stronger bond with you and Ray. Blessings on you and your family.

FOREWORD

By Meeke Addison

Inside each and every believer is the seal of our precious Holy Spirit. Because of this undeniable fact we have a power dwelling inside us that's inexpressible yet often untapped. As a result of our failure to tap into the ultimate source of our life we are empty desperate and ineffective.

On a daily basis we find ourselves wounded on the battlefield of our own mind. "Why don't things ever work out for me? When will things turn around? Is it ever going to be my turn?" Millions of people are plagued by thoughts just like these. What's worse is that followers of Jesus Christ are not in any better shape. We're haunted by failures and paralyzed by fear. God beckons us to follow His leading and we refuse. We're convinced that whatever we do is destined to bomb. Where does that thinking come from? Is it consistent with what we know about God? The truth is, it isn't.

In the book of Second Peter we learn from God's holy Word that God by "His divine power has given to us all things that pertain to life and godliness, through the knowledge of Him who called us by glory and virtue." So when our life stalls and we feel stuck we don't need another empty seminar. When we are convinced we can't handle one more door closed in our face, self-help simply won't help. If the Bible is accurate we have all we need to be successful in life and successful in pleasing God. Cortney understands this and that's why his book is unlike anything you've read before.

While every other book on the shelf intends to help you

help yourself, they can only take you to the point of temporary satisfaction. If they are not rooted in an understanding of how God has designed man and what He requires of us then they can never nourish the entire person. In "Stuck in Neutral" Cortney utilizes his experiences with the Lord and in life to help you truly live in drive. In the Kingdom of God there is no time for coasting. Ephesians teaches us to redeem the time because the days are evil; even admonishing us to find out what pleases the Lord.

God has given you all you need that pertains to life and godliness. It's time for us to tap into the "all" we've been given. No more sitting on the sidelines and coddling our regrets and failures. It's time to connect with the Lord and find out what pleases Him. And not just that it's time to do it. I thank God for the insight of faithful believers who are willing to spend themselves on behalf of the Gospel. I thank God for His sovereignty and faithful guidance, and I thank God that it's never too late to live in drive when you've been stuck in neutral.

1

MY JOURNEY TO LIVING IN DRIVE

My name is Cortney Sherrod Westbrook, and I was born in Columbus, MS. I want to show you how dedication, persistence, determination, sacrifices and courage play a part in your success, and I'm going to use my story to do so. I'm an entrepreneur, musician, author and radio host. I'm also an award-winning graphic designer.

A big imagination and creativity are two quality traits that every person should have–especially creativity. If you are not creative, you're probably not going to be very successful. If your plan A doesn't go the way you thought it would, you have to be creative enough to come up with a plan B off the cuff. However, my personal philosophy is that of something Will Smith once said: *I don't need a plan B because it distracts me from plan A.* Have a rock-solid plan, stick to it and stay focused; you can do anything you put your mind to do.

Over the years, I've successfully started four companies and three businesses, and every time I used the *No Plan B* philosophy. I never created a backup plan because I believe that says to your subconscious that you're not confident enough in plan A for it to work. Some people may disagree with me, and that's fine. The beauty about life is that there are many ways to be successful. My journey looks different from yours. What may work for me may not work for you.

The key is to find your lane and stay in it. Find what works for you and stick with it.

As a teen, I wanted to be an architect, and in high school I interned for a local architecture firm during the summer. I learned a lot during that internship that really sparked a desire inside me to pursue architecture when I went to college. However, during that same year–my sophomore year of high school–another desire was birthed inside of me. I have no idea where the desire came from, but I wanted to play the piano and be a musician. I told my parents, and when my dad bought me my first keyboard, I was totally stoked. I remember getting the keyboard and setting it up for the first time. I asked my dad what I was supposed to do with it, and he said, "Play it." So I did. I didn't have the slightest clue about what I was doing, but I had a determination to learn and that's all I needed. The first song I learned how to play was the famous "Fur Elise" by Beethoven.

Here's the lesson I want you to get from my experience: just because you don't know how to do something doesn't mean that you shouldn't try. A lot of people back away from their dreams because they've never done it before. They just shove it under the rug and forget about it. Did you know how to talk before you talked? No, but you tried anyway. Did you know how to walk before you walked? No, but you got up and tried anyway. Yes, you fell to the ground a bunch of times and probably even hurt yourself, but you didn't let that stop you. You kept pushing, you kept trying and eventually you walked. You didn't let your previous failures of falling stop you from trying. Channel the mindset you had as a child learning to talk or walk and use it to reach your success today.

Can you guess what happened when I started playing on

my first keyboard? Yep–I messed up. In fact, I messed up *a lot.* It didn't stop me, though; I kept trying and eventually learned how to play and was very good at it. I played for family, church and school, and eventually I became number-one in my college music courses and became known as the "big man on campus" in the music community. Why? Because I didn't let my fear of failure hinder my opportunities to succeed. I had a desire and I kept pushing.

Let's fast-forward to 2009. I got married, and upon my mother-in-law's recommendation, my wife and I started attending a church whose congregation included several business owners. That was the first time I encountered entrepreneurs, and they inspired me to eventually become one myself. Before then, I never thought about owning a business, and I never even knew I could because no one told me it was possible. Let me pause for a minute. I want you to catch two things here: I didn't see myself owning a business, and I never thought that I could because no one told me that I could.

You cannot do what you cannot see–not just seeing with your physical eyes, but seeing with your spiritual eyes. But wait, don't get it twisted; I'm not talking about any third eye kind of stuff. Humans are spiritual beings just as we are physical beings. So when I say spiritual seeing, I essentially mean mentally. You have to mentally visualize something before you can actually do it. One of my favorite movies is *The Waterboy* starring Adam Sandler. When he was playing football, the coach told him to visualize and then attack. It was funny, but also a powerful principle. Before you can be successful, you must see yourself as a success.

A lot of times we don't try things because we aren't sure we can do them. For example, my mom is an excellent cook, and she owned a soul food diner in Tupelo, MS. The only reason she started a business is because someone told her that she could. I worked at her diner for the duration of its existence, but I never thought that I could own a business myself because she never told me that I could. But what if she had?

So if no one has ever told you that you could own your own business, allow me to be the first. You can be a business owner. You can be a successful entrepreneur. You can be successful at whatever you want. It's really not as difficult as you may think. You just have to want it.

In 2010, when my wife and I were still newlyweds, our lives entered a dark place where no matter what we did, nothing worked. We were a classic case of what I call stuck in neutral. Due to unforeseen circumstances and one difficult life-decision, we were forced to move out of a five-bedroom house and back into my old room, upstairs at my mom's house. I was working a dead-end job, and Christian was working a temp job that was subject to end at any moment's notice. As a man, that completely crushed me. I mean, how was I going to be a good husband when I couldn't even provide a roof over my wife's head?

We spent countless days and nights arguing and disagreeing about everything from the smallest to the most important decisions. Needless to say, this was an extremely dark time for us, and we couldn't see even a shimmer of light. But just like with every dark place in life, there actually *was* light at the end of the tunnel. We eventually moved out of my mom's house and into our own. Christian found a better job, and I started my own business. Things looked a bit brighter, but unbeknown to us, 2010 wasn't the end of dark times; it was only the beginning.

There were times when I didn't know where my next client or paycheck would come from–when the lights got disconnected because we couldn't pay our bills–when I didn't have money to put gas in my car. You want to talk about stuck in neutral? Money got so tight for us that I once sold my car title for a low-interest loan and actually almost got the car repossessed for nonpayment. Whenever we took two steps forward, life knocked us five steps backwards. I had a business that I was drowning deeper and deeper in every day. On the outside, the appearances were picture perfect, but on the inside, it was a category-five hurricane. There were months when I had no idea how I was going to take care of my family. It got so bad that Christian threatened to leave me until I was able to provide for us. That's when I knew that we couldn't get any lower in life; we couldn't get any more stuck in neutral. We were textbook financially poor and were deteriorating faster than we could help it. There is no way I could give you every account of hardship, tragedy, tribulation and mishap we experienced, but I'll just say that I wouldn't wish what we went through on my worst enemy.

What we learned through that experience was the forging of character, patience, determination, long-suffering, peace and most important, complete reliance on God. On a personal development note, what we gained most through our struggle was HEART. Heart is something that can withstand any opposition you face in life. Heart can endure pain like nothing else in this world. When you have *real* heart, there's nothing that you can go through that you won't be able to handle. I've been through hurt, pain, loss, debt, abuse, struggle, slander, hate, betrayal and any other negative emotion or act that can be committed by or against a human. What brought me through it all is *heart*, the undying will to succeed and my faith in God. I always knew that I would be successful if I just made it through that one situation or that one hard time.

Everything that I have written in this book is what I have learned through my life's struggles, trials, tribulations, successes, victories and God-experiences. If you take these principles of success and apply them to your life, I *guarantee* you that you will be successful.

When a car is stuck in neutral it's impossible for it to move on its own. It can be the nicest, most expensive car on the market and have a tank full of gas–and you can press the accelerator all day–but until you put it in drive, it does you or no one else any good. Your life is the exact same way. And, if we're honest about it, we're all guilty of putting all of our emphasis on making our external bodies look impressive to other people, but we neglect the internal components and characteristics that make us who we are. Those that are successful are the ones that improve from the inside out. Put your life in the gear of drive by becoming the version of yourself who is capable of achieving success and living a full, happy life.

You've been living stuck in neutral for the majority of your life. Your life is in a state of paralysis, and no matter what or how hard you try, things just never seem to get better. Being stuck in neutral is when you experience constant unhappiness and un-fulfillment, not knowing why you're alive. God has created you for a purpose, but if you don't know what that purpose is and never live in it, then you'll never live the life you were meant to live. You'll always find yourself running in circles, trying to figure out life. But life wasn't meant to be figured out by us; God already has it figured out. All you have to do is put your life in the gear of drive and let Him navigate you to your destiny. So how do you put your life in the gear of drive? I'm glad you asked. Turn the page.

2

THE REAL WAY TO FIND YOUR TRUE PURPOSE

D espite how messed up you think your life is and despite how "stuck" you feel, there is a way to get out of neutral and get control of your life. This book is designed to help you fix the brokenness in your life–first by surrendering your life to God's plan, then by identifying your gift and discovering your purpose. The only *real* way to discover your purpose is to go back to your creator. No one on this earth can tell you what your purpose is. In fact, you can't even figure out your purpose for yourself. Some people refer to God as a "higher power" or "infinite intelligence", but let me be clear: God is the creator of all things and life. He created the universe, every planet and every human being on Earth. God is the only one who knows your purpose, and its discovery begins with a relationship with Him. If you do not have a relationship with Him, it's a very simple process to begin one. Romans 10:9 says, "If you confess with your mouth that Jesus is Lord and believe in your heart that God raised Him from the dead, you will be saved." To enter into a personal relationship with God, simply read this prayer:

Dear Lord Jesus, I know that I am a sinner. Please forgive me of all the sins I have committed against You. I believe that Jesus died on the cross for me and rose from the dead to sit at Your right hand. I accept Jesus Christ as my personal Lord and Savior. Come into my heart. Make me Your own. Help me to be the person that You created me to be. Reveal to me my life's purpose and strengthen and equip me to live it out on this earth. From this day forward, I commit my life into Your hands. I surrender my will for your will and my thoughts for your thoughts. Use me for Your glory. In Jesus' name. Amen.

If, with conviction, you read that simple prayer above, you have accepted Jesus into your life and now you can begin building a relationship with God. Angels are rejoicing in Heaven right now because of your decision to be a part of God's family. Please reach out to me and let me know that you made the bold decision to surrender your life to God. I would love to hear your testimony and give you free resources to strengthen your new relationship. If you ask Him, God will reveal to you the true purpose of your life. Then and only then, can you truly live life in drive.

Living In Drive!

LIVING A PURPOSE-DRIVEN LIFE

We were all born with some type of gift, talent or special ability. Your gift is a tool that will assist you in fulfilling your God-given purpose. Your purpose, sometimes referred to as calling, is what you were created to do. For too long, many people have had an identity crisis. Due to the lack of fathers in the home, a lot of children grow up not knowing who they are. Therefore, they turn to drugs, gangs and sinful lifestyles.

When you don't know who you are, it's impossible to know where you're going. If you don't know who you were created to be, you may be living someone else's design for your life. You may be living your boss' design for your life at a dead-end job. Don't get me wrong, there's nothing wrong with working a full-time job. However, not everyone is going to work a job that they love. You may not always be happy with your current place of employment, but while you're there, you should take every opportunity to maximize it and get the most out of it. Use it as a building block and driving force to push you towards your purpose.

When you don't know who you are, it's impossible to know where you're going. If you don't know who you were created to be, you may be living someone else's design for your life.

Along with purpose comes provision. See, you think that because you're the human living out your purpose on this earth, *you* are the one responsible for providing for that purpose. That's simply not true. God created you for a purpose, so He is the one responsible for providing for your purpose. When you live a life driven by purpose, you have no selfish needs, wants or desires. Why? Because everything you could need, God has it. Everything you could want and desire, He will give it to you if you are living according to His perfect will. And when you live in purpose, you are living in His will.

I have experienced this time and time again in my life. I know for a fact that I am living out my purpose on this earth according to God's perfect plan. Therefore, all of my needs are met. I want for nothing, and I can attain anything I desire. But that's not because I'm some great person who lives out my days looking down on others from my high horse. It's because I live in and ask according to His will and purpose for my life. Remember, right there in the middle of purpose is provision, but it all starts with a relationship. If you don't have a relationship with God, I implore you to begin one.

If you're starting a business based on your purpose, then you don't have to stress over getting funding, because God already knew you were going to need funding when He created you. So all you have to do is turn the engine on and let Him drive you where the funding is. I hope that makes sense, because *that*, my friend, is *living in drive!* This may be a little deep and sound foreign to you, but I promise, the more you read this book, the more you'll understand this.

It's important to understand this concept so that you can benefit from the principles outlined in this book. When you live in purpose, the walk will be easier because you're not doing it out of your own ability, but out of the ability with which God empowers you. Remember to never chase your purpose; live your purpose.

Living In Drive!

Learn to get in touch with the silence within yourself, and know that everything in life has purpose. There are no mistakes, no coincidences, all events are blessings given to us to learn from.

- Elisabeth Kubler-Ross

The purpose of human life is to serve, and to show compassion and the will to help others.
- Albert Schweitzer

Efforts and courage are not enough without purpose and direction.
- John F. Kennedy

I believe that God has put gifts and talents and ability on the inside of every one of us. When you develop that and you believe in yourself and you believe that you're a person of influence and a person of purpose, I believe you can rise up out of any situation.
- Joel Osteen

3

THE TRUE MEANING OF YOUR GIFT

A lot of authors, motivational speakers, TV hosts and life coaches will tell you that your gift will help you discover your purpose. I happen to disagree. Your gift isn't designed to discover your purpose; your gift is designed to be a tool that will help you fulfill your purpose. Your gift is not a tool of discovery, but a tool of fulfillment. In order to fulfill your purpose, you must first know what it is.

God has given everyone a specific gift, though some people have multiple gifts. Question: if you have multiple gifts, does that mean you have multiple purposes? Answer: no; you have one purpose. Just because you're gifted at something doesn't mean that's the reason you were put on this earth. I, for instance, have the gift of music and the gift of design, but those gifts/skills will not discover my purpose. My gifts are simply vehicles that will give me the capacity to fulfill my purpose.

Your gift is your supernatural ability to do something. It is a special power that gives you the capacity and capability to function beyond what is considered normal or natural. Your gift is something that you do the best without having to try very hard. It's that thing that people always ask you to do and marvel at you when you do it. It's that thing that no one else can do the way you do it. It's that one thing that you will do for free!

Your gift is a tool that God has given you to help you fulfill your purpose. Your purpose is the overall reason you were put on this earth. Simply put– it's the reason God created you. Your gift is something that you can do. Your purpose is much bigger than your gift. I don't believe that your gift will necessarily lead you to discovering your purpose. I believe that your gift is an indication of the fact that you were created for something that's much bigger than you. We were all put here for a purpose that is bigger and much more important than what we can physically do.

You were created for greatness and you will accomplish greatness through your supernatural ability. You will accomplish greatness through a specific tool that God has given you. You will fulfill your purpose through the use of your gift.

Living In Drive!

A winner is someone who recognizes his God-given talents, works his tail off to develop them into skills, and uses these skills to accomplish his goals.

- Larry Bird

I want to challenge you today to get out of your comfort zone. You have so much incredible potential on the inside. God has put gifts and talents in you that you probably don't know anything about.
- Joel Osteen

DISCOVERING YOUR GIFT

The worksheet on the next page is designed to help to identify your gift. **These are 10 questions you should ask yourself when identifying your gift.** Whatever consistent answer you have for these questions is more than likely your God-given gift. In the next section we will discuss what your gift is and how to maximize it.

10 QUESTIONS TO ASK YOURSELF WHEN IDENTIFYING YOUR GIFT

1. What are you passionate about?

_____

2. What do you often find yourself daydreaming about?

_____

3. What do people always ask you for or ask you to do?

_____

4. What is it that you can "do with your eyes closed"?

_____

5. What is it that you do that causes you to lose track of time?

_____

6. What makes you feel the happiest?

_____

7. What will you do for free?

_____

8. What makes you feel incomplete if you don't do it?

_____

9. What do you think people will pay you for?

_____

10. What do you want to be remembered for after you've passed away?

_____

UNDERSTANDING YOUR GIFT

Your gift is a tool that will assist you in fulfilling your purpose. It is a skill that God gave you when He created you. It is that thing you excel at doing without giving much effort, and you are most fulfilled when you do it.

gift–God-given ability that gives you the capacity to function beyond what is considered to be normal or natural

Again, your gift is something that you can do. It's a talent or a skill. Simply put, your gift is your supernatural ability to perform. This may be redundant, but I want to make sure you understand this and don't get it confused with your purpose. And since your gift is something that is given to you by God, it cannot be earned or taken away from you.

Has someone ever given you a gift that you didn't like, so you never used it? It just sat under the counter or was tucked away in the back of a drawer. Well, just because you don't use it, doesn't mean that it goes away. Your God-given gift is the same way. No matter how much you don't want it, how little you recognize it, or how deep you bury it within your soul, it will never fade, never disappear and never cease to exist. It is something that was innately woven into the fabric of your DNA during your creation. If you're not using your gift, you're more than likely not fulfilling your purpose, because your gift is designed to help you fulfill your purpose. Despite popular belief, your gift will not discover your purpose. Your gift is a tool of fulfillment, not of discovery.

Your God-given gift gives you the capacity (internal ability or competence) to do something beyond what is normal or natural according to society's standards or common sense. It is your supernatural ability to perform an action. Since you're only human, a natural third-dimension being, you may be wondering how you can do something supernaturally. And that's a great observation. The only way you can do something beyond what seems to be natural is with God's empowerment. When you operate in your gifting, God puts His super on your natural. I like to think of it as a special power. You have this special ability to do something that no one else in the world has the capacity to do. You can do things that no one else can do, and they marvel at the way you do it. Sure, other people can have the same gifting as you, but no one can do it the way you do it. It is a unique ability, meaning only you can do it that way.

When you step into prideful competition, you step out of gifting and you cease to fulfill purpose. You cannot compare purpose by competing with gifts.

Keep in mind that it's important for you not to become boastful of your gift, because it is just that–a gift. You didn't work for it, earn it, or buy it, so you don't have the right to be boastful about it. When people don't understand that, they get into using their gifts for competition. There's nothing wrong with innocent competition, but prideful competition is dangerous. You must realize that you're not better than someone else because you can do something they can't; that just makes you unique, different. When you step into prideful competition, you step out of gifting and you cease to fulfill purpose. You cannot compare purpose by competing with gifts. Be confident in your God-given ability and what He has called you to do, and you'll automatically be successful.

God has created you for a purpose and given you a gift. And you do yourself a disservice if you never use it to fulfill your purpose. He has called you to do something, and until you know what that is, you will forever be stuck in neutral. I'm sure this goes without saying, but you've been stuck too long. You've merely existed too long. You've been "just trying to make it" for too long. Now is the time to shift gears and maximize your potential by living life in drive.

Living In Drive!

4

THE SECRET TO GETTING AHEAD IS GETTING STARTED

I once heard an acronym for the word NOW: No Opportunity Wasted. You can't wait until the "right time" to step out there. You can't wait until you think you know the right step to make. The next step is the right step, because as long as you are stagnate, it'll be difficult or even impossible for you to reach greatness. NOW is the right time to start that business. NOW is the right time to go back to school. NOW is the right time to pursue your dreams and live your God-given purpose.

I'm here to tell you that if you never step out and pursue your dream, you will never have a dream come true.

You don't have to know all of the steps before you get started. Did you know the entire alphabet before you started singing the song? Probably not. I'm here to tell you that if you never step out and pursue your dream, you will never have a dream come true. Don't worry about where you are and what you have. Don't let your present situation define and dictate your future success. Don't let your past failure doom your future success. Use what you have until you can get what you want and need. Do what you can do until you can do what you want to do. The key is to just act NOW! Don't let any opportunity go to waste.

Let me ask you this one question: What's under your feet? Weeds or wind? Don't let weeds grow where you're standing. Let wind carry you to your next leap of faith. You need to be moving so the only thing under your feet is wind. Go out there and live in drive!

Living In Drive!

5

DON'T BELIEVE IN YOURSELF

Yes, you did read the title right. Don't believe in yourself. Before I tell you why you shouldn't, though, allow me to encourage you for a moment.

You are your biggest fan and your worst critic. If you keep that mindset, you'll be successful. When you're up crying in the middle of the night and no one is there to wipe your tears, you have to wipe your own tears and know that God hasn't left you. When you're going through a rough patch in life, you have to lean on God's strength instead of the people that you thought were going to be there for you. When your friends and loved ones don't support you, you must support yourself. Yes, I know that's easier said than done, but all successful people have the mindset that if no one else wants them to succeed, they want success for themselves so badly that they will make whatever required sacrifices to get there. Sometimes you'll have to talk to yourself. Tell yourself that you did a good job; thank yourself; tell yourself to stay focused. It may sound weird and unorthodox, but I know from experience that it actually works.

What I've learned, though, is that God is really the only person that will always be there for you. He will never leave you or forsake you.

All of that self-help motivation I just gave you in the

second paragraph is great, but it's only mumbo-jumbo if you try to do it alone. So don't believe in yourself, believe in God. Don't try to figure out life on your own; He already has it figured out. All you have to do is put your life in the gear of drive and allow Him to navigate you to your purpose. I talk about confidence in the next chapter; and it is great information, but don't put your complete confidence, reliance and dependence in yourself, put it in God. So once again, don't believe in yourself, believe in God because we sometimes let ourselves down, but God will never let us down.

The advice I'm about to give you is the best piece of advice that I can ever give you.

The key to all of my success is: knowing that I alone am insufficient, and without the help of God, I would not be where I am today. Everything I do, every word I say and every letter I type, I do it with the strength and the leading of the Holy Spirit. My advice to you is to quickly get to the end of yourself. The quicker you get to the end of your rope, the quicker God can step in and take your life to the next level. The quicker you get to the end of yourself, the quicker you can tap into the supernatural (God's strength and ability). If you allow it, God will put the *super* on your *natural* and you will do supernatural things on this earth. People will marvel at "your ability" and ask how it is that you do what you do, and you will tell them that it is only by God's grace, strength and

If you can dream it, you can do it. If you can think it, you can do it. If you can see and imagine it in your mind, you can do it. See yourself successful, and then go be successful.

26

ability that you are who you are and where you are today.

If you can dream it, you can do it. If you can think it, you can do it. If you can see and imagine it in your mind, you can do it. See yourself successful, and then go be successful.

Living in Drive!

Now unto him that is able to do exceeding abundantly above all that we ask or think, according to the power that worketh in us.
Ephesians 3:20

I can do all things through Christ which strengtheneth me.
Philippians 4:13

Private dreams are the most powerful. You have to dream of success to make it happen, and if you don't believe in yourself, nobody else will. But that doesn't mean you have to go around telling everyone about it.
- Tony McCoy

6

GUARANTEED SUCCESS WITH GOD-CONFIDENCE

You can accomplish what most people see as impossibilities. All you need is confidence – *God-confidence*, to be more specific. If you want to be wildly successful, put your confidence in God, not man. Don't put your confidence in your job. Don't put your confidence in your 401k. Even though this entire book is about personal development, don't even put your confidence in *self. Real* success starts with the God kind of confidence.

Let me tell you something: when I meet with business clients, often times they automatically give me their business because of the confidence I exude. They have no idea that it's not *my* confidence I exude; it's the God-confidence that's on the inside of me. When I open my mouth to speak, they hear *His* confidence come out. When I walk into the room, there's a trail of confidence following me that affects every person I come in contact with. Look, it's not about me and I know that. It's not about *my* ability or *my* handsome looks (I just had to throw that in there); it's all about the confidence that I've put in God to do what I need done. *He* empowers me to be who I am and do what I do. On my own I am as insignificant as they come. I'm just a whacko trying to make it through this life. But *with* Him, I'm a BEAST! *With* Him I'm a force to be reckoned with. Listen to me, when this principle is in operation in your life, it puts you in a place where you can ascend to levels of success and accomplishment you never even dreamed about. You will ascend to levels of greatness you never thought possible.

Whatever you want to accomplish in life, you can do it. If you want to accomplish those things that seem impossible, you can do it. All you need is the right formula. And here it is:

Now this is the confidence that we have in Him, that if we ask anything according to His will, He hears us. And if we know that He hears us, whatever we ask, we know that we have the petitions that we have asked of Him.
1 John 5:14-15

God is only obligated to His word, not yours. The scripture above basically says that if you ask God anything according to His will, with confidence, He hears you and you will have what you ask of Him. When you live life in drive by living life in purpose, you are guaranteed success. When you live your life in the purpose that God created you to live, everything you do should line up with that purpose, which is His will. And whatever you ask Him for that's according to His will and His purpose for you, you will automatically receive it. Now that sounds awesome, right? But wait... as true and accurate as that is, here's the catch: it's not always going to be easy and it's not always going to happen that way *you* want it to. Once again, if it was easy everyone would do it. It may not be on your timing or

Whatever you want to accomplish in life, you can do it. If you want to accomplish those things that seem impossible, you can do it. All you need is the right formula.

turn out the way you want it to, but if you put your confidence in God, you can accomplish the impossible and success will be guaranteed. That's God-confidence. In the next chapter, you will learn how you can develop confidence to become successful.

Living In Drive!

Now this is the confidence that we have in Him, that if we ask anything according to His will, He hears us. And if we know that He hears us, whatever we ask, we know that we have the petitions that we have asked of Him.
1 John 5:14-15

7

BUILDING SUCCESS WITH CONFIDENCE

S uccess can be attained through confidence. But if it doesn't come natural to you, don't worry because it's like a skill– it can be learned and developed. The process of developing confidence can help you conquer the fear that has made you unconfident; you just need to take action and do the work. It doesn't come easily, but it also doesn't come without a great reward. If you're not a naturally confident person, it takes work for you to develop it; but again, it's not impossible. Take small steps towards building your confidence. Take your time and do it right. If you want to be successful, you must first understand a few things about confidence.

Confidence is not based on your status. It's not based on your gifts and ability. As hard as it may be to believe, it's not even based on your good looks. Confidence is based on who you are on the inside and then that's displayed on the outside. It's also not based on what you have. You can be the richest person in America, have a Fortune 100 company or have the largest church in the world, but that doesn't mean you will automatically be confident.

Confidence is based on who you are, not what you possess. Though it's also not based on what you are able to do, your ability *can* help increase your confidence. However, it is not *determined* by your ability. For example, I'm a musician. I play bass guitar, saxophone and keyboard as my main instrument. I've played in gospel bands, country bands, stage plays, churches, campfires, recitals, and tons of other venues. When I was in college I was the "big man on campus" when it came to playing keyboard. The thing is though, I wasn't an amazing player. I didn't know all of the music theory that a lot of the others knew; that's actually why I was in college– to learn theory. I wasn't a piano phenomenon. But the thing that set me apart was my confidence and my musicianship.

Being a musician is more than just knowing how to play some notes. Being a musician is a mindset, a discipline.

Remember, confident people are secure, so they don't feel the need to compare or compensate for anything. They just accept their shortcomings and try to make them better.

You can be an awesome musician, but if you don't have confidence when you play, you will make mistakes, get frustrated and have a poor performance. But if your confidence level is where it needs to be, then you can be a mediocre musician like I was and use that confidence to have an outstanding performance. That's what I did and it has been working for me ever since then, in other areas of my life. I never compared myself to other musicians because I was confident in my own skin.

An important thing you must learn about confidence is that it will always be damaged by comparison. When you compare yourself to other people, you feed your insecurities. Comparison is the thief of all joy because it makes you feel that you are insufficient compared to other people. And on the other end of that same spectrum, comparison can make us think more highly of ourselves than we ought to think (Romans 12:3). All in all, comparison feeds that part of us that we see as weakness, which in turn makes a major blow to our confidence.

Confidence is a required, essential ingredient if you want to be successful in any area of your life. Come on and be honest, when was the last time you accomplished something that you didn't truly believe that you could? It just doesn't happen very often or at all. If you're not confident and optimistic, how will you be successful? Successful people are confident and they know it. Don't get it twisted; being confident is not arrogance. If you think about it, the people who accuse others of being arrogant usually suffer from a lack of confidence themselves. Those who are arrogant try to cover their lack and insecurities with blame and never taking personal responsibility. Remember, confident people are secure, so they don't feel the need to compare or compensate for anything. They just accept their shortcomings and try to make them better.

If you've ever heard that confident people take risks, then you heard right. They're not afraid of the unknown. They're also not afraid of experiencing failure. Those who know that failure is inevitable are those who will be successful. It's also true that people with low confidence never take risks. Because they're not confident in their ability to do something, they will never take the risk and try. As a consequence, they will never be successful. Are you that person?

So how exactly do you build confidence? Well, start with small changes. Small changes make a big difference. With action comes more confidence. The more you act on your dreams, the more confident you are in pursuing them. The more you practice your gift, the more comfortable you are in performing it. This principle is all about taking action. Action generates confidence. Confidence generates action. The more you act, the more confidence you have. The more confidence you have, the more you act, and eventually the more you accomplish.

Confident individuals are comfortable publicly sharing their achievements. They don't mind addressing a public audience. At the same time, they're also comfortable sharing their mistakes and failures, because they know that in those mistakes and failures are gemstones of success. Those that are confident and successful maximize their strengths and improve their weaknesses. If someone criticizes you of something you said or did, take that as an opportunity to improve yourself. Don't get angry. Don't let that temporary criticism of failure negatively affect your confidence and potential success. See, just because you failed doesn't mean you're a failure. The very fact that you tried means that you had some level of success, even if it was learning how *not* to do it. Failure means that you can do better; take it as a positive thing.

Understanding and developing confidence can be a funny thing. Sometimes, when you go out and do the thing you're most afraid of, the confidence comes afterwards. It's like jumping out of a plane and hoping that the parachute will open on the way down. You just have to take action.

Living In Drive!

I can do all things through Christ who strengthens me.
Philippians 4:13

Let us therefore come boldly to the throne of grace that we may obtain mercy and find grace to help in time of need.
Hebrews 4:16

Believe in yourself! Have faith in your abilities! Without a humble but reasonable confidence in your own powers you cannot be successful or happy.
- Norman Vincent Peale

8

LIVING A LIFE OF GRATITUDE

Being consciously grateful is essential to a happy life. Gratitude keeps you positive and optimistic, which are two important characteristics for a person to have. You should never forget that you get what you give, and being a positive person will bring more positive people, events and opportunities into your life. I truly believe that a grateful attitude opens doors for more opportunities of thankfulness. This has proven true in my personal life time and time again. I can think back to times when I didn't have anything to be grateful for–or so I thought. When I was stuck in neutral, I didn't know that my attitude of hatefulness toward my negative situation only bred more of the same situations that I hated.

It took me going through hell to see that my situation wasn't going to change by the attitude I possessed. I decided to make a shift in my mindset, which ultimately made a shift in my life. Right now you may be dealing with some of the same challenges that I dealt with; and I'm here to tell you that all you have to do is change your perspective. If you don't like what you see then change how you see it. If you don't like the fact that all of your needs aren't met then start being thankful for your needs that *are* met. If you don't have all that you want, start being grateful and thankful for what you *do* have and you'll see the little turn into an abundance. If you're ready, let's explore how to develop a mindset of gratitude.

Living in Drive!

Develop an attitude of gratitude, and give thanks for everything that happens to you, knowing that every step forward is a step toward achieving something bigger and better than your current situation.
- Brian Tracy

Gratitude is the healthiest of all human emotions. The more you express gratitude for what you have, the more likely you will have even more to express gratitude for.
- Zig Ziglar

Be Thankful

If you woke up today with the things you thanked God for yesterday, what would you have? "Thank you" is the greatest prayer that you could ever pray. Those two words, when said with a truly genuine heart, display the greatest degree of humility.

Look around you. No matter who you are, you've got something to be thankful for. Look, it doesn't matter what kind of house you live in; be thankful that you have a home. The roof over your head, the health that allows you to wake up every morning, your job, your family and friends, and the

If you woke up today with the things you thanked God for yesterday, what would you have? Thank you is the greatest prayer that you could ever pray.

food you eat are all things to thank God for every day.

For some people, the harsh reality is some of those things are privileges. So often we overlook the small things. Running water, for instance, is something we take for granted because it's so common to us. In America we may drink half of a bottle of water then pour the rest down the drain or leave it on the counter, while people in other countries are dying because of the diseased, contaminated water they have no choice but to drink. The things that are so rare to other people have become so common to us that we actually devalue it. The next time you want to pour an unfinished bottle of water down the drain, think about the people in other countries that die because they don't have the very thing you discard. The next time you want to complain about what you don't have, think about the people living on the streets with nothing. I've met some of those people before and to be honest, they are more grateful than we are. And that's because they know that gratitude isn't determined by what they possess. True gratitude is determined by your attitude.

So I ask you again, if you woke up today with the things you thanked God for yesterday, what would you have? The more you're thankful, the more there is to be thankful for. I need you to understand this–it's all about perspective.

Humility breeds gratitude and gratitude breeds humility. Likewise, ingratitude breeds selfishness. People who are selfish are not generally humble people. The more you think about your insufficiencies, the more you want. The more you want, the more you seek to obtain. So make sure that you're thankful for everything that you've been blessed to have. You may not have all that you want, but if you honestly believe that there is nothing to be thankful for in your life, you're blind. If you are reading this right now, you can be thankful for your eyes and your mental capacity to understand the words on this page.

If you're not grateful for what you have, you won't likely get anything that's worth having. You can continue to toil and labor all of your life, but without gratitude, you will always be stuck in neutral. A sure-fire way to live life in drive is to be grateful and thankful every day of your life. Thank God for the small things. If you are thankful for what you have, you'll see that you have more than enough to be thankful for.

Living in Drive!

'Thank you' is the best prayer that anyone could say. I say that one a lot. Thank you expresses extreme gratitude, humility, and understanding.
- Alice Walker

TURN NEGATIVES INTO POSITIVES

Viewing every negative you encounter as a positive will help you live a life of gratitude, and gratefulness makes turning negatives into positives very easy. The thing is, though, as children some of us weren't taught to be grateful, so as adults it doesn't come easily. Some people were taught to be brats, and others were taught to do whatever it takes to get what they want, even if that requires dishonesty or using and stepping on other people to get to the top. But in reality, those are guaranteed pathways ways to emanate failure.

Next time you feel like complaining, be grateful instead. When you feel like complaining about your job, be grateful that you have one. When you want to complain about your children acting up, be grateful that you have children to raise; some people will never know what it feels like to be a parent.

Your level of gratitude shapes your attitude. And vice versa. It's all a domino effect. How grateful you are will be displayed in your actions. Your heart will be reflected in your actions, but it all starts in the mind. If you can change the way you think about life, your life will change. Bottom line: have a mindset of gratitude and watch your life shift from neutral to drive!

Living in Drive!

Everything negative - pressure, challenges - is all an opportunity for me to rise.
- Kobe Bryant

APPRECIATE CHALLENGES

A person is not defined by what happens to him in life; a person is defined by how he deals with and responds to his circumstances. I've heard that life is 10% what happens to you and 90% how you respond to it. Life is going to happen, so you will always have challenges. The question is not *if* the 10% will come; the question is how will you respond to the 10% when it does?

What does your 10% look like today? What are those challenges that you must face? What are those hurdles that you must overcome? And what does your 90% look like? Will you react to the 10% or respond to the 10%?

Although different, reactions and responses are reflections of your character. A reaction is a subconscious behavior that occurs without your permission. A response is a calculated and well-thought out action. Which one occurs depends on the quality of your character. You have a choice whether to react or respond.

You also have the choice to let your challenges break you or make you. I do understand that bad things happen to people, but you should use those bad things to your advantage in becoming a better person. With every challenge you face, there is a life lesson to learn. With every suffering you endure there is growth and strength in the struggle. When you are weak, God becomes your strength (2 Corinthians 12:9-10).

Be grateful for the opportunity of challenge. Enduring challenges is the path to growth and becoming a stronger person–You 2.0! You will face some periods of challenges and sufferings that you will simply have to outlast. It doesn't last always though. Suffering doesn't last always. Darkness doesn't last always.

When you're in a dark place of life, remember that it's only temporary and you can get through it. You were meant to go *through* challenges, suffering, pain and darkness–not be filled with it.

I once heard an illustration about boats and ships. Boats and ships were designed to navigate through water. But if enough water gets inside of a boat, it will sink. Now, apply that same principle to your life. If you allow the challenges, suffering, pain and darkness to fill you, before long, you will sink and perish. That's called being stuck in neutral. When you allow what you're going through to get inside of you, you will sink and become defeated. You were never created to be filled with darkness, pain and struggle; you were created to overcome it. And that, my friend, is living in drive.

Living in Drive!

Accept the challenges so that you can feel the exhilaration of victory.
- George S. Patton

LOVE EVERYONE

⁷ Beloved, let us love one another, for love is of God; and everyone who loves is born of God and knows God. ⁸ He who does not love does not know God, for God is love. ⁹ In this the love of God was manifested toward us, that God has sent His only begotten Son into the world, that we might live through Him. ¹⁰ In this is love, not that we loved God, but that He loved us and sent His Son to be the propitiation for our sins. ¹¹ Beloved, if God so loved us, we also ought to love one another.
1 John 4:7-11

The Holy Scripture commands us to love one another just as God loved us. God is all about love. Does that mean you will *like* everyone? Probably not. Will everyone like you? Those chances are even slimmer. There is no way you're going to like everyone, just like there is no way everyone is going to like you. But you *can* love everyone. If God loves, and if we were created in His image and likeness, that means that we must love as well. Moreover, if we as humans didn't have the capacity to love, the Bible wouldn't have instructed us to do so. When we love people, we have a deeper appreciation for them and for life. Love breeds gratitude.

Every person who comes into your life can teach you something. Every time a new person comes into my life, I ask God, "Why? Why are they here? Why did I meet them? What do they have to do with my destiny?" It may sound weird, but it's true. If you know why people are a part of your life–whether they're there to teach you something about them, the world, or yourself–it makes it easier to be grateful for them.

And because we are imperfect, we will mess up and we will offend one another. But I submit to you today that it is so much better to love those who offend you than it is to hate them. Now, if it was easy, everyone would do it. It's going to be difficult, but the reward is great. When we love, we live. Only when you are grateful for the people in your life will you truly love them and find joy.

Living in Drive!

[30] And you shall love the Lord your God with all your heart, with all your soul, with all your mind, and with all your strength.' This is the first commandment. [31] And the second, like it, is this: 'You shall love your neighbor as yourself.' There is no other commandment greater than these.
Mark 12:30-31

[34] A new commandment I give to you, that you love one another; as I have loved you, that you also love one another. [35] By this all will know that you are My disciples, if you have love for one another.
John 13:34-35

TREASURE LIFE'S MOMENTS

Treasure every moment that life brings your way–no matter how big or small, no matter how important or insignificant, and no matter how frequent or infrequent. I've talked a lot about preparing for the future and the things that are to come. By all means, you should do that. But in your preparation, don't miss the NOW. Don't miss the moment that is right in front of you. Life is only but a moment. One day it's here, and the next it's gone (1 Peter 1:24-25). So we have to protect it, appreciate it and be grateful for it.

Treasure every single moment that you have; you never know when you won't have any more left. Treasure every moment that you have with your family, your spouse. Treasure every moment that life brings you. I've experienced a lot of deaths in my family, and during those times I've learned to treasure the people in my life.

I grew up with my cousin, Darren. We were two peas in a pod. We were raised together and graduated high school together. April 11, 2009, I traveled to Indiana to marry my wife. But, Darren couldn't travel because of his bad health. He passed away that weekend before I could make it home to see him. Months later, his mom suddenly passed away. Needless to say, that was a very dark time in my life. But it was also a turning point for me. From that moment forward, I vowed to live life in the moment and always cherish family and relationships.

Quit worrying over your problems, and just live. We all have things we're dealing with and struggling through, but be grateful that you are alive. Live life in the happy moments, and quickly learn from and get over the bad. Each moment in which you take the time to be present will help you garner a deeper appreciation for life. Be grateful.

Living in Drive!

Life is not measured by the number of breaths we take, but by the moments that take our breath away.
- Hitch

9

NO SACRIFICE, NO SUCCESS

In order to be successful, sacrifice is required. Where there is no sacrifice, there is no success. Where there is no sacrifice, there is no growth. God made the ultimate sacrifice by sending His beloved Son, Jesus Christ, to the earth to be crucified and die on a cross for mankind. And because of God's sacrifice, we now are able to have eternal life; we are no longer relegated to sin.

So if God, the creator of the universe, had to sacrifice His Son so that we could live, what is it that you must sacrifice in order to be successful? Where there is no sacrifice there is no success.

sac·ri·fice

1. the act of giving up something that you want to keep especially in order to get or do something else or to help someone

2. destruction or surrender of something for the sake of something else

3. something given up or lost

Sacrifice, as seen above, is defined as the act of giving up something that you want to keep in order to get or do something else or to help someone–giving up something to get something. That's the principle. You have to give up your mindset of failure in order to gain the mindset of success. You must give up your time in order to be successful. You must give up your fleshly pleasures in order to get from where you are to where you want to be. You must give up being stuck in neutral in order to live in drive. You must destroy every negative, debilitating mindset that you have. You must surrender to God your natural life on this earth in order to live an eternal life in Heaven.

Sacrifices are not convenient. I get up at 4:15 every morning. Do you think that's convenient for me? Do you think that's easy for me all the time? It's not. It's not going to be convenient for you to make the necessary changes in order to become the person you want to be; that's why they're called sacrifices. You will have to give up something that you don't really want to give up. And here's the slap in the face: it won't be easy. Giving up something *Without maturity, you will always be too selfish to give up what's required.* you love for something that will yield greater results is not going to be a brisk walk in the park. However, it's required. If there is no sacrifice, there is no success.

Every sacrifice must be something of value in order to receive something of greater value. Sacrifice requires maturity. Without maturity, you will always be too selfish to give up what's required. But don't fret. There is light at the end of the tunnel. There is always a positive outcome in sacrifice. With great sacrifice comes great victory. In the Bible, Abraham was willing to follow God's command and sacrifice his only son, Isaac. Do you think that was easy for Abraham to do? It wasn't. But, his sacrifice was of great value. Nevertheless, he was willing to do it. And because of his father's willingness, Isaac was spared and Abraham became the father of many nations. The parallel is when God sacrificed His Son, Jesus. Because of that, all of mankind received the opportunity for eternal life.

So I ask you this question again: what are you willing to sacrifice in order to be successful?

Living In Drive!

10

MAKE ADJUSTMENTS, NOT EXCUSES

The word adjustment holds two principles that I want to extract. Principle 1 is Adjust Me, and Principle 2 is Just Me. When you make excuses, the person that is affected most is you. You're the only one responsible. Make adjustments, not excuses. When you make excuses, you excuse yourself right out of the way. You excuse yourself right out of the open door that's in front of you. You excuse yourself right out of what God has for you. You excuse yourself right out of every opportunity that could be available to you.

"Well I don't have the money. I don't know how to do that; I've never done it before. I didn't grow up with money in my family. My dad wasn't there. I'm a college dropout."

All of those are excuses.

I, for example, grew up in a family that didn't have much money. My dad wasn't a consistent part of my life, and I'm a college dropout. But, you don't hear me making excuses for any of that. I made adjustments, not excuses.

So, let's jump into the principles.

Principle 1: Adjust Me –When there is an external problem, make an internal adjustment.

When there is something wrong or not going the way it should go, adjust yourself. Don't look at others like they're the problem. Don't blame other people for your failure. If you've had failure in your life, you're the one who's ultimately responsible for it. You often want to blame others for your problems, lack of finances, lack of a job, lack of peace or lack of opportunities. Yes, there may have been some bad circumstances that you couldn't avoid; I'm not talking about those situations because I understand that. However, at the end of the day when you lay your head down on your pillow, you are the one who's ultimately responsible for how you respond to what happens in your life. And that brings me to the next principle.

Principle 2: Just Me –You are personally responsible for every success and failure in your life.

Personal responsibility is the greatest responsibility there is –take it. Make adjustments, not excuses. When I fail at something, it's just me. When I have to stand before God, who is going to be up there? No one. It's just me. So, I can't point the finger at other people because of my lack of performance.

Don't look at other people to blame for your lack of knowledge. Crack open a book. You've heard it said before that if you want to hide something from a Black man, put it in a book. It's time to kill that, not only in the African American race, but in *every* race and nationality. It's time to destroy ignorance. You need to first embrace your ignorance by accepting that you are ignorant and that you do not know. Then you need to eradicate your ignorance with the application of knowledge and learning.

Knowledge is not power. Knowledge is *potential* power. Knowledge only becomes power when it is applied. You can know how to build an engine. You can know how it works inside and out, but until you apply that knowledge by putting the engine in a car and connecting all of the wires and pumps, your knowledge is useless. Unless you apply your knowledge by teaching someone else what you know, you're not using your knowledge to its maximum potential.

Don't blame other people for your problems. Don't pass the buck to someone else and say that it's someone else's job. Take personal responsibility for your life. When you make the necessary adjustments to become successful, you will then become a success. Make adjustments, not excuses.

Living In Drive!

11

PROBLEMS ARE NOT STOP SIGNS, THEY'RE GUIDELINES

W e all know that the stop sign was created to tell drivers when and where to make a complete stop. It prevents you from having accidents on the road and keeps you safely inside of the car. Problems are not stop signs; they're guidelines. Problems don't tell you to stop, they give you indications of how to proceed to your final destination.

If you've ever driven on a major highway, then you know about the large green signs that indicate how far away from the next destination you are. They also indicate what lane you need to be in and when you need to take an exit that will lead you to where you're going. Problems are exactly the same. When you encounter a problem, it may indicate that you should be in the left lane or that you should take the next exit. They may tell you that you're 15 miles from your final destination. Problems keep you on the right track by telling you to make slight adjustments to your route.

However, until you change your perspective about problems, you will always give up because you perceive them to be stop signs. You must change your perspective in order to change your perception. If you don't like what you see, then change how you see it. If you can't change what you're looking at, then change how you look at it. Don't stop when you encounter problems; learn from them and keep living in drive.

Years ago, I met an older businessman who had a lucrative car wash and detail business. He started the company when he was younger and living in California, before he and his wife moved to Atlanta, GA. They live directly across the street from well-known rapper André Lauren Benjamin, better known as André 3000. As the older businessman and I were sitting in his sunroom by the tennis courts, I asked him what the key to his success was, and he said something so profound, yet so simple, that I will remember and live by it as long as I'm in business.

He said, "Young man, all you have to do is just stick around. If you can stay in business longer than your competition, you will be successful. I've seen businesses come, and I've seen businesses go. There have been other car wash businesses that started around here, but they didn't last. I'm on top because I outlasted them. The reason a lot of people don't succeed is because they keep giving up. Just don't quit, and you'll make it. Hang in there." Those simple words of wisdom have kept my engine running ever since.

Yes, you will fall, but even if you fall on your face, you're still moving forward. Even if you have to crawl, you're still moving forward.

I want to encourage you to keep moving forward. Yes, you will make mistakes and bad decisions. Yes, you will fall, but even if you fall on your face, you're still moving forward. Even if you have to crawl, you're still moving forward. I know you'll get tired if things get darker and more difficult, but if you just hang in there and don't quit, you will reach success.

Living In Drive!

Our greatest weakness lies in giving up. The most certain way to succeed is to always try one more time.
- Thomas A. Edison

12

NEGATIVE + POSITIVE = POWER

It takes a negative and a positive to create power. Let's look at a car for example: the battery features the red charge, which is positive, and the black charge, which is negative. When you connect a pair of jumper cables to the battery, both the negative and the positive are needed to jumpstart another battery; one charge doesn't work without the other. If the negative is connected and the positive is not, then nothing happens. And vice versa. Only when both connections are made will the electrical current pass through the cable to what's on the other end. Only when both are connected will power flow from the battery through the cables.

If you look at your life just the same, you will see the parallel. If you're a positive person, then you actually need a negative person to balance you out. Without negativity, there would be no need for you to be positive in the first place; there would be nothing to combat. See, all negative people have to do is rub you the wrong way to create a spark–just like the jumper cables.

When you change your perspective on haters, you will see them for what they really are. They are the other side of the cables necessary to create power. When your haters pop their heads up and start speaking negatively about you, that should give you a spark of power that will recharge your whole mindset. Gain energy from your haters. They will always be there, so why not utilize their energy to your advantage? And just so you know, haters don't know their purpose. That's why they hate on you when they see you fulfilling yours.

You will always have someone who doesn't like you–that's a part of the journey of success. Just remember that it takes a negative and a positive to create power. And if you're a negative person, you must have a positive influence in order to get anywhere in life. Just think about it.

Living In Drive!

13

Understanding Failure

Don't Let Fear Keep You from Trying

D on't let the fear of failure keep you from doing your best. Fear of failure will keep you from giving your 100 percent. If you're honest, the fact that you failed at something before makes you apprehensive about doing it again, and that's because you don't want the same results that you got the last time. However, the very fact that you tried and gave 100 percent effort means that you succeeded. It means that you're a success.

Many people actually never step out there and try, which makes them failures. Do not be afraid of what may happen if you try; be afraid of what *won't* happen if you don't try. You may never reach your maximum level of success if you never give it a shot.

Wayne Gretzky once said, "You miss 100 percent of the shots you don't take." So, my question to you is, would you rather have 100 percent of failure or 10 percent of success? It's entirely up to you.

On a similar note, Coco Chanel said, "Success is often achieved by those who don't know that failure is inevitable." I would disagree with that. I submit that success is achieved by those who *do* know that failure is inevitable. In order to reach success, you must know that failure is all a part of the journey. The quicker you jump off the cliff of failure, the sooner you will soar in the sky of success. Also, when you step out there and fail at something, your response matters. You have a small window to decide what you will do. What you do with failure will determine if you're a failure or a success. When you reach the door of failure, you have two choices: 1) accept the failure and become a failure, or 2) learn from the failure and become a success. I pray, my friend, that you choose the latter. I want you to take failure and feed it to your success. Let failure be fuel to the fire.

Living In Drive!

It's fine to celebrate success but it is more important to heed the lessons of failure.
- Bill Gates

Sometimes by losing a battle you find a new way to win the war.
- Donald Trump

Failure will never overtake me if my determination to succeed is strong enough.
- Og Mandino

It is impossible to live without failing at something, unless you live so cautiously that you might as well not have lived at all, in which case you have failed by default.
- J. K. Rowling

THE CLOSER YOU GET TO FAILURE

When you fail, you gain knowledge on how *not* to do something the next time. When Thomas Edison was trying to create the light bulb, he failed at least 10,000 times before he found the right formula. But he was determined to succeed because he knew the right answer was somewhere inside of him. He knew that at any given time, he could be only one formula away from the right one. And it only takes one.

It's simple. The quicker you get to failure, the quicker you get to success. The closer you get to no, the closer you get to yes. And remember, a no doesn't mean never; it means this isn't it. It means this person isn't the right one. It means this job isn't the right job. It means this opportunity or business isn't the right one. The more *NOs* you get, the closer you get to your yes.

You can't appreciate a *yes* until you get a *no*, because when you don't know what *no* looks like, you will never know what a *yes* looks like. And because you don't know, a *no* could in fact be a *yes*. But because you have no idea of what a *no* is and you have no experience of a *no*, you could, in fact, miss the *yes!* It's the same way when something is given and not earned. You can be given something and not know its value, but it's impossible to earn something and not respect its value.

I could give you $10,000, and if you don't know the value of that money, you will waste it faster than you can say your ABCs. Then as you look around, wondering where it went, you'll have absolutely nothing to show for it. On the other hand, if you earn $10,000 on your own, there is nothing in the world that anyone can do to make you waste that money, because you understand and know the value of it. Give a man a fish, feed him for a day. Teach a man to fish, feed him for a lifetime.

Living In Drive!

NEGATIVE EFFECTS OF FEAR

Fear paralyzes you. Fear will make you stagnate, control your thoughts and dictate your actions. It creates indecisiveness that results in immobility. Do you know someone who is talented or gifted in something, but they won't utilize that talent or gift? I believe we all do. Those people will procrastinate indefinitely on using their gift rather than risking failure. Fear of failure will paralyze you and make you lose out on opportunities that are right at your fingertips. Lost opportunities cause erosion of confidence, and the downward spiral leads to being stuck in neutral.

Fear creates bad habits. One of the things that determine your quality of life are your habits. Your life is a direct reflection of your habits. Fear can become a bad habit, and the only way to get rid of a bad habit is to replace it with a good one. The only way to replace a habit of fear is with the habit of risk. Don't be afraid to take risks. Taking risks builds your faith, builds your confidence and strength.

Fear steals joy, peace and confidence. When you're consumed with fear, you're not living as happily as you should; and you're not as enthusiastic about life. The erosion of fear may start in only one area of your life, but it will soon spill over into other areas. After a while, it becomes who you are and everything you do will be done out of fear.

Fear creates an atmosphere of chaos that causes you to always be on edge and nervous. Fear breeds fear. It is a seed that you plant, and you know what happens when you plant a seed–it grows. When you plant the seed of fear, you will reap a harvest of fear, and it will be greater than what was actually planted. The crop is always greater than the seed.

Fear creates doubt. This is probably one of the most debilitating effects of fear. It makes you doubt yourself and your ability, which in turn will paralyze you, causing you to be stuck in neutral.

Living In Drive!

For God has not given us a spirit of fear, but of power and of love and of a sound mind.
2 Timothy 1:7

I've learned that fear limits you and your vision. It serves as blinders to what may be just a few steps down the road for you. The journey is valuable, but believing in your talents, your abilities, and your self-worth can empower you to walk down an even brighter path. Transforming fear into freedom - how great is that?
- Soledad O'Brien

PAIN IN FAILURE

Every failure can be associated with pain. That's why people turn to alcohol, drugs, food addictions and other vices–to try and numb the pain of their failure and overbearing distress. What they don't realize, though, is that drugs and alcohol are only artificial, temporary reliefs. When that high wears off, the fear and the problems are still there. When they come off the hangover, the issues they tried to escape still reside.

One thing about fear and failure is that you cannot cover them up. You cannot sweep them under the rug. So don't try to cover up fear with artificial, temporary relief because it will not go away; it will only get worse.

Living In Drive!

14

THE REAL KEY TO SUCCESS

People who want to know what it takes to be successful read books, go to seminars, workshops and pay monthly retainers to life coaches–all to hear the same information about success. Everyone seems to think they have the key to success, but real, divine success only comes from following God's plan and purpose for your life.

If I told you that God has a formula that guarantees success for anyone who follows it, would you be interested? Well, I'm going to give you the formula to be successful God's way. Of the two types of success–good success and bad success–we obviously want good success. And this success formula is found in the Bible.

This Book of the Law shall not depart from your mouth, but you shall meditate in it day and night, that you may observe to do according to all that is written in it. For then you will make your way prosperous, and then you will have good success.
Joshua 1:8

Basically this passage says that if you meditate on God's Word day and night then do what it says, you SHALL be prosperous and you SHALL have good success. That word

SHALL is one of, if not the, strongest words in the Bible. When you see that word, whatever follows it means that it's guaranteed to happen, exactly the way the scripture says.

Do you remember those ads and commercials that said, "There's an app for that" –meaning someone has created a mobile app for anything you can think of? Well, the scripture is the same way. Anything that you may encounter and go through in life, *there's a scripture for that.* There is nothing on this earth you can face that isn't found somewhere in the Bible. As it relates to success, all you have to do is take the Word of God, apply it to different areas of your life and watch the results come to pass. It is honestly that simple.

Living In Drive!

15

OVERCOMING OPPOSITION AND NEGATIVITY

D oes the slightest opposition or resistance discourage you? Do you fail to achieve your dreams because you always expect and want it to be easy? You need to know that you will likely encounter some form of resistance with whatever you want to achieve in life. It may come in various forms and at times from unexpected or unusual places or people.

The Laws of Nature: Gravity and Friction

Newton's third law of motion says that for every action there is an equal and opposite reaction. There's good and bad, strength and weakness, happiness and sadness, success and failure, rich and poor, problem and solution. The decisions you make today will affect you later. It may not be immediately, tomorrow or even next week, but your decisions will affect you at some point in your life. That's why you must be conscious and aware of your decisions.

If you want to be successful, you must first overcome the friction and gravitational pull of negativity. Opposition pushes away from success and attracts you to itself. Just like in the natural sense of the word, gravity is an attractive force that pulls any and everything towards it with no discretion. However, if there is anything that I've learned, it's that the gravitational pull of opposition strengthens you. In order for you to walk and jump, your physical muscles have to develop the strength to overcome gravity.

When astronauts go into outer space, where there is less gravity and friction, their muscles and bones become weaker, so much to the point where some astronauts can't walk for some time after they return to Earth. Without the opposition of gravity and friction, their bones and muscles actually deteriorate.

In order to succeed, your mental, emotional and spiritual muscles have to develop the strength to overcome gravity. There is no way around that; without gravity and friction, you won't succeed, but deteriorate. As crazy as it may sound, without opposition, there is no forward progression.

Opposition is defined as anything that is in direct contrast with your goals and journey to success. When someone hates on you, that's opposition. When the devil is coming against you and shooting darts, that's opposition. Will you put up a shield of faith (Ephesians 6:10-18) and continue the fight, or will you cower down and be defeated? It's your call.

Living In Drive!

REQUIRED RESISTANCE TO OVERCOME

If you want to be successful, resistance is required. Body builders use resistance to make them stronger, build and tone muscle and make them look and feel good. Resistance tests your belief, drive, determination, persistence, consistency and strength. It is a true test of what you're made of. Your greatest form of resistance will not come from other people, things, society, financial struggles or negative circumstances. Your greatest form of resistance will always come from within. You are your greatest form of resistance. You are your worst enemy, and until you become okay with that and learn how to handle YOU, success will always be a fleeting idea.

Not only are you your greatest source of resistance, you are also your greatest asset. That's why you should spend countless hours, days, months and years improving yourself. No one on this earth is perfect, but you should still strive to be. Don't concern yourself with what other people are doing and saying. Focus on you and your God-given purpose. You are your worst enemy and your greatest asset. Live accordingly.

Living In Drive!

RESOLVE TO OVERCOME

I've said several times in this book that what happens to you doesn't matter, but what you do about what happens to you does. Trials and tribulations will come until the day you expire, but you must make a conscious decision that you will overcome whatever you face. Make up your mind that you will not let negativity control you or get the best of you. In order to *live in drive*, you must have a burning resolve to not only continue doing what you're doing, but to do it even better and to strive even further. When you're faced with one of life's fires, be encouraged, inspired and motivated to do more, press deeper and grind harder. ET says don't cry to give up, cry to give more. You're already in pain, why not get a reward for it?

Let the negativity and opposition you experience strengthen and forge you into the machine you need to become in order to reach success. Sometimes negativity and opposition is exactly what you need to become better. Eat them like an energy bar. Don't let the stones that people throw at you break you. Instead use those stones to build a wall of fortitude –an impenetrable force. Don't lose focus! Make up in your mind that you WILL overcome!

Living In Drive!

Opposition is a natural part of life. Just as we develop our physical muscles through overcoming opposition - such as lifting weights - we develop our character muscles by overcoming challenges and adversity.
- Stephen R. Covey

Adversity has the effect of eliciting talents, which in prosperous circumstances would have lain dormant.
- Horace

WELCOME CHALLENGES

One of the things I've learned in my 27 years of living is that if you are not challenged, you cannot grow. Challenge is the required water that your roots need to grow deep. As backwards as it may sound, if there is nothing to push against, you cannot make any progress. I heard a quote once that stuck with me: *"A smooth sea never made a skillful sailor."* How will a sailor learn to sail without rough winds and waves? The fact is he won't.

If you're absolutely satisfied with your life, then fine—close this book right now and go do something else. But, if you know that there is more to life than just living... if you know that there is another level of success for you to reach, I want you to dig way down deep inside of yourself and yank out the will to change and succeed.

Most of the time positive change must come as a result of some negative influence that forces you to change. It's rare that positivity causes you to change. If you tell me that I'm doing a good job and to keep up the good work, then there's really no red flag that says I need to do anything differently. On the other hand, if you tell me that it's not working, I'm going to figure out how I can make it work. It's simple. So, welcome challenges. They equal change and opportunity for growth.

Living In Drive!

LOOK FORWARD TO THE HATERS

I talk quite a bit about haters because I've experience my fair share of them in my life, and I've learned that you must always be prepared for that kind of opposition. The haters and naysayers would love to see you fall. They will lie about you, steal from you and betray your trust–all for your demise. Friends make the worst enemies because not only is it upsetting to be betrayed by a friend, but it's also hurtful. Hurt people tend to hurt people.

I've gotten it figured out though. Here's why someone would want to stop someone else from being all that they can be: because they (the haters and naysayers) aren't being all that *they* can be. Because of their insecurities and failures, they don't know how to handle anyone else's success. And because they failed, they don't want to see other people succeed. Misery loves company, remember?

The definition of a hater is someone who does not know his or her purpose. If haters and naysayers knew their purpose, they would be so busy fulfilling it that they wouldn't have time to hate on you for fulfilling yours. Haters like to tell you that you can't do something because they can't do it.

When I wanted to start my first business I shared my dream with someone very close to me. They told me that I couldn't do it and that I should focus on working a job. They told me that it wouldn't work. That hurt me really bad because I valued this

Because of their insecurities and failures, they don't know how to handle anyone else's success.

person's opinion and I thought they had my best interest at heart. It hurt me so much that it motivated me. Now, to be fair though, I did understand why they told me that. I was married, working a dead-end job and living with my mother. Life was extremely bleak and dark for us at the time, but I had the desire and will to succeed. Although, my circumstances screamed NO, my dreams screamed YES. See, your dreams must be louder than your circumstances. Your dream must be louder than the haters that tell you that you can't or shouldn't do something. Listen to your dreams, not your haters.

Don't ever let anyone tell you that you can't do something. The fact that they're telling you that you can't, actually means that you can. Use their negativity and hatred as fuel on the fire. Nothing encourages me to take action more than someone doubting me.

There will always be someone who doesn't like what you say, what you do, your beliefs or even small petty things like how you wear your hair. My response to that is this: SO WHAT! Other people's hatred simply signifies that you're on the right track. You can't live your life to please everyone because you will always fail to do that. If you live your life to please God, you will attain and become the ultimate success that you desire.

Living In Drive!

Using Negativity to Your Advantage

When you're met with opposition, it's important for you to not give up. Your will to succeed should be greater than the will to be rid of the negativity. The objective is to endure opposition until the end because there is great reward for your struggle. I've learned that you will encounter some opposition and resistance that you just have to outlast. You're going to go through some stuff that you can't get out of, but you just have to never give up in it. I'd rather attempt to do something great and fail than to attempt to do nothing and succeed. I never want to be successful at doing nothing. The reality is, though, you won't pursue success because you're afraid of failure. You don't want to try because you already believe that you can't do it. Confucius said, *"The man who says he can and the man who says he cannot are both correct."* The tougher the conflict, the more glorious the triumph. The more opposition, the greater the victory. It won't be easy, though. ET says that if it was easy, then everyone would do it.

If it were easy, you wouldn't have resistance, and everyone would love you all the time. If it were easy, it wouldn't be a real victory. And my favorite: If it were easy, failure wouldn't scare you. Think about it.

This is your moment–seize it. This is your time–maximize it. This is your opportunity–make it count. This is your life–do something with it. You only get one life on this earth, so make the best of it. Don't live life merely existing... *LIVE LIFE IN DRIVE!*

LIVING IN DRIVE AFFIRMATION

Living in drive begins with a mindset and translates into a lifestyle. It all starts with the mind. You must make up in your mind today that you will live in drive. So, every morning I re-sight this affirmation:

"From this day forward I'm going to live a life of joy and freedom. I can and will be successful. I will accomplish all of the impossible things that I have told myself I could never do. I am no longer going to be bound by my past mistakes; and I will not be controlled by fear. God has created me for a purpose and I will live the rest of my life being the person that He wants me to be."

TAKE ACTION

Now that you've read the entire book, I want to encourage you to take action on what you've learned and apply it to your life. As you've learned, success has a lot to do with your life in many areas. There are 6 areas of your life that you should always be focused on making better:

1. Personal (development, habits)
2. Family (children, extended family)
3. Relationships (marriage, social)
4. Work (finances, business, job)
5. Health (physical, exercise)
6. Spirituality (religion, mentality)

Take a serious look at each of these areas and set goals, make plans and pray, meditate and think on. If you want to change your life, it starts with you taking action. No one is going to do it for you. So, stop being lazy and complacent and put in the necessary work. If you want success like you've never had before, you must do, think, speak, believe, pray, work and grind you never have before. GO!!

GET CONNECTED

1. Join Cortney's mailing list
2. Listen to the Up Together radio show, weekdays at 12 noon central on Urban Family Talk
3. Receive inspirational text messages from Cortney
4. Subscribe to Cortney's YouTube channel for motivational videos
5. Follow #inspo365 for inspirational and motivational quotes
6. Follow Cortney online:
    a. Facebook.com/cswestbrook
    b. YouTube.com/cortneywestbrook
    c. Instagram & Twitter @cswestbrook
    d. Pinterest.com/cswestbrook1

Get connected online at www.cortneywestbrook.com and www.livingindrive.com.

ABOUT THE AUTHOR

Cortney Westbrook is a husband, radio host, author and musician. He's passionate about empowering people to fulfill their God-given purpose. Having started four companies and three businesses, he understands people and has made it his life's work to serve others–so much so that he is beloved as "The People's Entrepreneur."

Cortney is published author of two books, including self-help book *Stuck In Neutral* and music education book *Beginners Guide to Music Theory*. In his spare time he allows his passion for music to flourish. He has released five music projects with more to come. Cortney is also a national radio host and can be heard daily on Urban Family Talk, a radio division of American Family Association. For encouragement and motivation, catch him weekdays as host of "Up Together" and for unapologetic commentary on currents events, catch him on Urban Family's morning show, "Airing the Addisons." Cortney's vision in life is to motivate and inspire people to live life to its fullest. His favorite quote is "Let's make it better by living in drive together!"

To Contact the Author

Mail: Attn: Cortney Westbrook

PO Box 2251

Tupelo, MS 38803

Phone: (662) 205-6378

Email: cortneywestbrook@gmail.com

Website: www.LivingInDrive.com

www.CortneyWestbrook.com

www.UrbanFamilyTalk.com

29229510R00063

Made in the USA
San Bernardino, CA
16 January 2016